Great Sporting Events

by Serena Ramsay

Contents

Introduction

Great sporting events give athletes the chance to test themselves against the world's best. They also give spectators the chance to see the world's top athletes in action, to see their strengths and weaknesses.

Some of us may be lucky enough to watch these events live, while others watch on television.

For many athletes, success in a world-class sporting event can be very rewarding. Sports are now a multi billion-dollar industry. The very top athletes earn millions of dollars. But athletes sometimes risk their lives trying to become the best in the world. Sometimes the danger is very much part of this appeal, not only for the competitors but the spectators, too.

Chapter 1
The Olympic Games

It's hard to imagine that a sporting event that was first held thousands of years ago still has such a lasting impact today. Back in ancient Greece, only men were allowed to take part, and the winners were given an olive branch. Things have changed since then, but the name is still the same—the Olympic Games.

The modern Olympics began in Greece in 1896, and today are held every four years in a different city around the world. At the first modern Olympics, there were 311 competitors from 13 countries, and women were not allowed to compete. In Sydney, Australia, for the 2000 Games, more than 11,000 athletes from 199 countries competed in 33 different sports.

The closing ceremony at the Olympic Games in Sydney, 2000.

? DID YOU KNOW?

The youngest Olympic medalist was an unknown French boy between seven and ten years old. He was on one of the Dutch rowing crews in 1900. The oldest medal winner was Oscar Swahn from Sweden. In 1920 he won a silver medal at age 72!

The athletes from each country parade around the stadium at the opening ceremony of each Olympic Games.

Olympic Traditions

There are a number of *symbols* and traditions associated with the Olympic Games.

The Olympic *motto* is written in Latin and means: Swifter, Higher, Stronger. The Olympic flag shows five interlocking rings in blue, red, yellow, green, and black. These colors were chosen because all the national flags in the world include at least one of these colors.

The Olympic flame stays lit throughout the Games and is only put out at the closing ceremony. Before the start of each Olympics, a torch is lit in Greece at the site of the ancient Olympics.

In 2000, after arriving from Greece, the Olympic torch began its Australian journey in Uluru, Central Australia. The torch was carried all around Australia before arriving in the host city, Sydney.

The Olympic flag is raised at the beginning of each Olympic Games.

The torch is then carried by many
runners, in a relay, to the host city.
If there are very large distances
to cover, the torch is
taken by airplane.

Winter Olympics

The Winter Olympics were first held in France in 1924. They are held every four years, but not in the same year as the summer Olympics. Events include figure-skating, speed-skating, skiing, bobsledding and ice hockey.

The Paralympics

The Paralympics are international games for the physically and, more recently, the mentally disabled. They are held in the same year and city as the Olympics. Events include wheelchair basketball, swimming, *archery,* and track and field. Like the Olympic Games, the Paralympic Games have their own symbols and traditions, including the Paralympic flame and flag.

Wimbledon

Wimbledon is the most famous tennis *tournament* in the world. It is held at the All England Lawn Tennis and Croquet Club in Wimbledon, a suburb of London, England.

The first tournament was held more than a hundred years ago, in 1877. It was played on grass, the same surface that is used today. In the beginning, only men were allowed to enter. Seven years later women were permitted to play.

Wimbledon is held every year in June. Hundreds of thousands of spectators watch the matches at the courts, and millions of tennis fans all over the world watch the tournament on television.

Martina Hingis in action at Wimbledon.

Wimbledon Champions

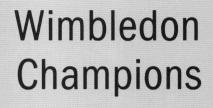

The singles finals are usually held on the second weekend of the tournament. The women play on Saturday, and the men's final is on Sunday. Both matches start precisely at 2:00 pm. For the winners, it is a very special victory. No other tennis title is more rewarding than a Wimbledon championship.

There have been many great Wimbledon champions over the years. American Pete Sampras has won Wimbledon seven times. He is nick-named 'Pistol Pete' because of his powerful serve, and he shares the all-time record with William Renshaw, who won seven titles in the 1880s.

Martina Navratilova won a record nine Wimbledon women's singles titles during the 1970s and 1980s.

Martina Navratilova

London: Sunday, July 9, 2000

SAMPRAS GRABS ALL-TIME WIMBLEDON RECORD!

American Pete Sampras has re-written the record books with his victory in today's Wimbledon men's singles final. The win gives Sampras a total of thirteen Grand Slam titles, one more than the previous record held by Australian Roy Emerson.

Twenty-eight year old Sampras overcame an ankle injury to defeat Australia's Pat Rafter in four sets (6-7, 7-6, 6-4, 6-2) over 172 minutes, with the match twice interrupted by rain.

The victory was even more special for Sampras, because his parents were watching from the stands. It was their first visit to Wimbledon, and the first time they had seen their son win a Grand Slam title.

Sampras must now surely be considered one of the greatest tennis players the world has seen. Even he doubts that his record will be broken.

"Well, time will tell if it will be broken. I think in the modern game, it could be quite difficult. It's a lot of commitment and a lot of good playing at big times."

The win gave Sampras his seventh Wimbledon singles title, to add to his Grand Slam tally of four US Open titles and two Australian Open victories. Only the French Open at Roland Garros has eluded this champion, and no doubt Sampras will try hard to rectify this slight blemish on the record books in the near future.

Chapter 3

Tour de France

Imagine getting on your bike one morning and riding for almost 125 miles. Then cycling that far again the next day, and the next day—in fact, for the next three weeks! This is what cyclists do in the world's greatest cycle race, the "Tour de France."

The race is held each year in July. It is usually staged in France but sometimes part of the race is held elsewhere in Europe. The course varies each year, but it always includes several very tough mountain stages, and is about 1900 miles long. Time trials are also included, in which the riders sprint over a certain distance.

More than 200 riders compete in the race, but many do not finish. Injury, spectacular crashes, and fatigue make this race very demanding.

The leader at the end of each day wears a yellow *jersey*. He continues to wear it until there is a new leader.

? DID YOU KNOW?

Only three riders from English-speaking countries have won the Tour de France. They are Americans Greg LeMond (a three-time winner) and Lance Armstrong, and Ireland's Stephen Roche.

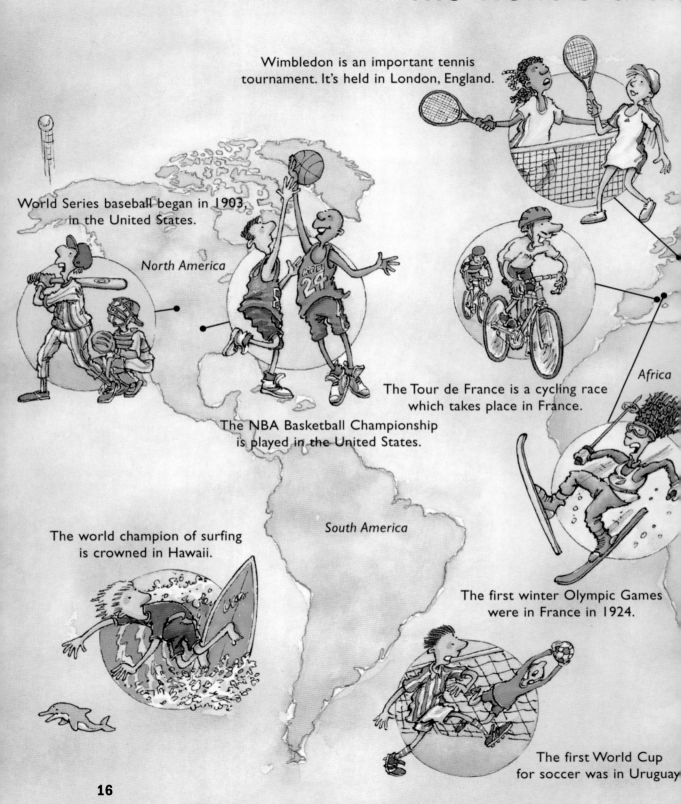

Wimbledon is an important tennis tournament. It's held in London, England.

World Series baseball began in 1903 in the United States.

North America

The Tour de France is a cycling race which takes place in France.

Africa

The NBA Basketball Championship is played in the United States.

The world champion of surfing is crowned in Hawaii.

South America

The first winter Olympic Games were in France in 1924.

The first World Cup for soccer was in Uruguay.

16

Sporting Events

The British Open is the oldest golf tournament. It is often played in Scotland.

The ancient Olympic Games were held in Greece more than 2000 years ago. The first modern Olympic Games were held in Athens, Greece in 1896.

One competition for the world championship in surfing is held in Japan.

Europe

Asia

The first Paralympic Games were held in Rome, Italy.

The first World Cup for rugby was played in New Zealand and Australia.

World Cup cricket is played every four years, in different countries.

Australia

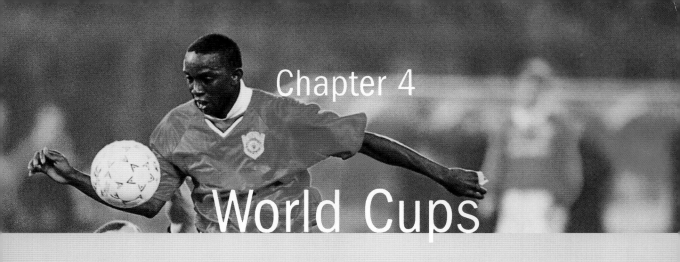

Chapter 4

World Cups

In some sports, the biggest and best event is the Olympic Games. In others, it is a World Cup or World Championship. These are usually held every four years in different cities around the world.

World Cup Soccer

Soccer is one of the most popular sports in the world. The most important international trophy for soccer players is the World Cup.

The first World Cup was held in Uruguay in 1930. Since then, Brazil has won the Cup four times, and Germany and Italy have each won it three times.

More than 170 countries play qualifying matches. Then the top 32 teams take part in the World Cup matches, which are played over a month's time. Millions of spectators attend the matches, and billions of viewers from around the world follow it on TV.

Huge crowds follow their team's progress in the World Cup.

![?] **DID YOU KNOW?**

Pele, from Brazil, is the most famous soccer champion. He is the only player to have won three World Cups, in 1958, 1962 and 1970.

Rugby World Cup

One of the world's newest sporting events is the rugby World Cup. The first World Cup was held in Australia and New Zealand in 1987. The winning team is awarded the Webb Ellis trophy.

There is great *rivalry* between the nations that compete in the World Cup. More than 60 countries try to qualify for the World Cup, but only 20 teams play in the actual event. The top four nations are Australia, New Zealand, South Africa, and England.

? DID YOU KNOW?

Before the start of each match the All Blacks, from New Zealand, perform the "haka." This Maori tradition is like a war dance and is very loud. It is meant to scare the opposition, even before the first whistle has been blown!

World Cup Cricket

The World Cup is the trophy for the best team in "one-day" cricket. "One-day" or limited overs cricket was once called "the pajama game" because players wear brightly colored clothing and often play at night under lights.

The first World Cup was held in 1975. Back then, just six countries competed. Now, the top twelve cricketing nations gather every four years to compete. These include Australia, New Zealand, England, Scotland, South Africa, Bangladesh, the West Indies, India, Pakistan, Sri Lanka, Zimbabwe, and Kenya. About two billion people watched the 1999 World Cup on television.

Australia beat Pakistan to win
the 1999 World Cup,
which was played
in England.

Chapter 5

NBA Championship

It is known as the toughest, meanest, and most highly paid basketball competition in the world. Welcome to the National Basketball Association, better known as the NBA. The NBA began in 1947 and the Philadelphia Warriors were crowned the first champions.

The competition is held in the United States, but the teams include players from all over the world. Most players are very tall, and the sight of a 6'5" tall player is quite common. Some are even taller!

Twenty-three teams are divided into two *conferences*. The NBA season is a long one for the players. Each team must play almost a hundred games in its quest to be the NBA champion. Each year, at the end of the regular season, the top teams in each conference have a *play-off* series to determine the championship.

Michael Jordan is one of the most famous basketball players in history. He played for the Chicago Bulls and led his team to six championships.

Chapter 6

Surfing: The World Championship Tour

For many of us, the thought of riding a surfboard on a 25 foot wall of water is sheer terror. But this is what the world's top men and women surfers face when competing on the World Championship Tour.

The Tour is held over twelve months at the best surfing beaches around the world. The top 45 men and 15 women are invited to compete. There are twelve World Championship events, and the surfers gain points from each event. The surfer with the most points at the end of the year is crowned the world champion.

Kelly Slater was crowned world champion six times in the 1990s.

Lisa Anderson was the women's surfing champion five times.

The World Tour starts in March in Australia, then moves to Tahiti, Fiji, South Africa, California, France, Spain, Brazil, and Japan. It ends with the crowning of the world champion in Hawaii.

Chapter 7

The World Series

Mention the name New York Yankees and baseball fans everywhere will recognize it. It is the most successful team to have competed in baseball's World Series.

World Series baseball began in the United States in 1903. Boston was crowned the first winner. Then they were called the Boston Pilgrims. Now they're called the Boston Red Sox.

There are thirty major league clubs in America. They belong to either the National League or the American League. Each league is divided into three divisions. At the end of the season, the three division winners—plus the runner-up with the next best record—play off for the right to compete in the World Series.

The top two teams then play a series of seven games to determine the world champions. To be the winner a team must win four of the seven games.

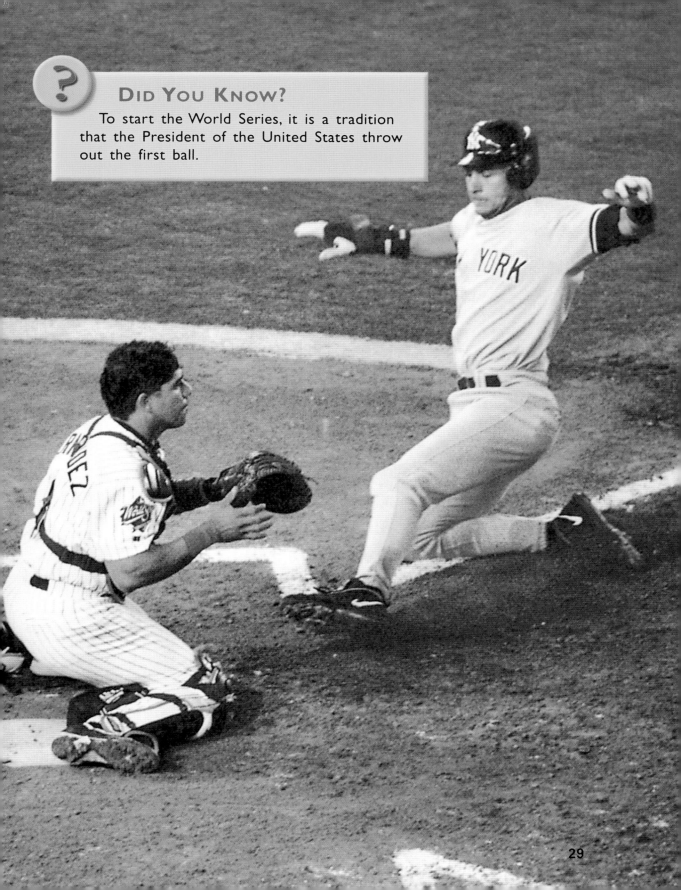

?

DID YOU KNOW?

To start the World Series, it is a tradition that the President of the United States throw out the first ball.

Chapter 8

Golf's Major Tournaments

Where would you find a "Tiger" and a "Shark" playing together? American Tiger Woods and Australian Greg "the Shark" Norman are two great golfers who both play at the major tournaments. Four events make up the "majors": the British Open, the US Masters, the US Open, and the US PGA (Professional Golf Association).

The British Open is the oldest tournament. It was first played in 1860, and is held each July in Scotland or England.

The US Masters is played each April at the same course, the Augusta National Golf Club. Entry to the tournament is by invitation only, and the winner is presented with a green jacket. The US Open is held each year in June and the US PGA in August, on courses throughout America.

The challenge for players such as Tiger Woods is to make history and win all four golf tournaments in one year. It hasn't happened yet.

Tiger Woods is one of the greatest players in the world, and he's only in his twenties.

The green jacket is awarded to the winner of the US Masters.

Glossary

archery	a sport using a bow and arrows
conferences	groups of teams in basketball
jersey	the long-sleeved shirt worn by the winner of each daily stage in the Tour de France
motto	a saying
play-off	an extra series of games to decide the winner
rivalry	the competitive spirit that occurs when two teams or people compete for the same thing
spectators	people who watch a sports event
symbols	signs or objects that have special meaning
time trial	when the competitors race against the clock
tournament	a sporting competition